The Gingerbread Man

Retold and activities by Lisa Suett
Illustrated by Valeria Valenza

Young ELi Readers

Before you read

1 **Look and write the words below the pictures.**

old woman • cottage • (to) catch • old man
oven • gingerbread man • cow • across
horse • fox • river

2 Can you make a gingerbread man? Match the verbs to the pictures.

1 ☐ roll
2 ☐ cut
3 ☐ decorate
4 ☐ mix
5 ☐ bake

a 

b 

c 

d 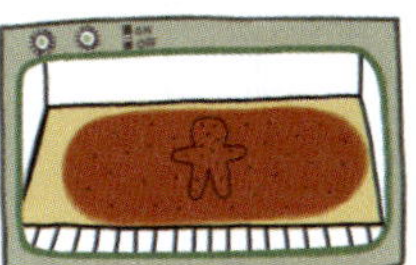

e 

▶ 2 An old woman and an old man live in a cottage.
The old woman is in the kitchen. She's making a gingerbread man.

What do you need to make a gingerbread man? Look and tick.

- [ ] butter
- [ ] sugar
- [ ] milk
- [ ] ginger
- [ ] apples
- [ ] flour
- [ ] eggs
- [ ] pears

The gingerbread man has got a head. He's got two eyes. He's got a nose and a mouth. He's got arms and legs.

3 The old woman puts the gingerbread man in the oven.
But soon she hears...

The old woman opens the oven door.
The gingerbread man jumps out and runs across the kitchen.
He runs across the living room... the bedroom... and the bathroom.
The old man can't catch him.

Write the names of the rooms.

kitchen • bedroom • bathroom • living room

STOP!

4 'Stop!' says the old man. 'Come here! We're hungry. We want to eat you.'

But the gingerbread man doesn't stop. He runs and runs and sings...

5 *Run, run, as fast as you can.*
You can't catch me, I'm the gingerbread man!

6 The gingerbread man runs and runs. Soon he sees a cow.

'Mooo!' says the cow. 'Come here. I'm hungry. I want to eat you.'

But the gingerbread man doesn't stop. He runs faster. The cow runs after him. The gingerbread man sings…

7 *Run, run, as fast as you can.*
You can't catch me, I'm the gingerbread man!

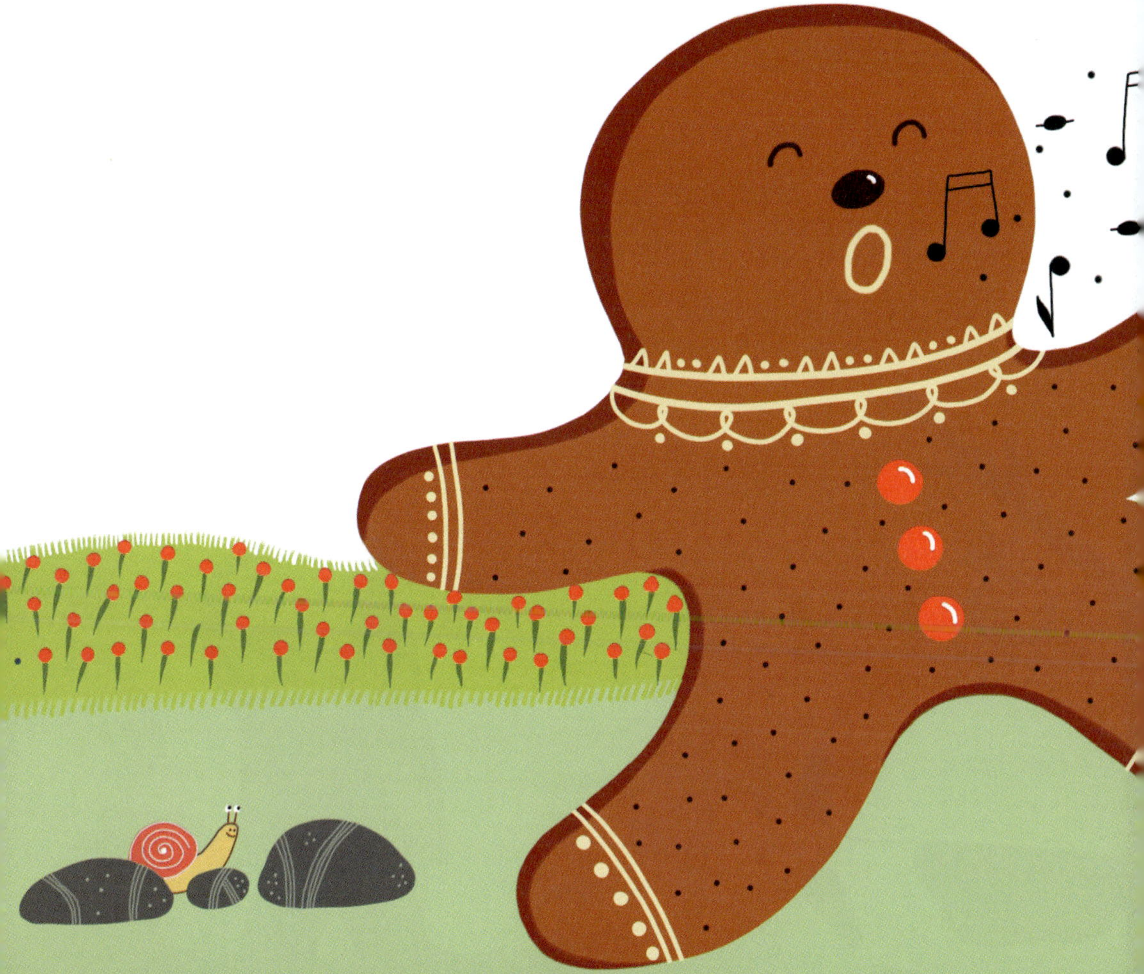

The gingerbread man can run. Match these actions to the pictures.

skip • jump • clap • hop • climb

1

2

3

4

5

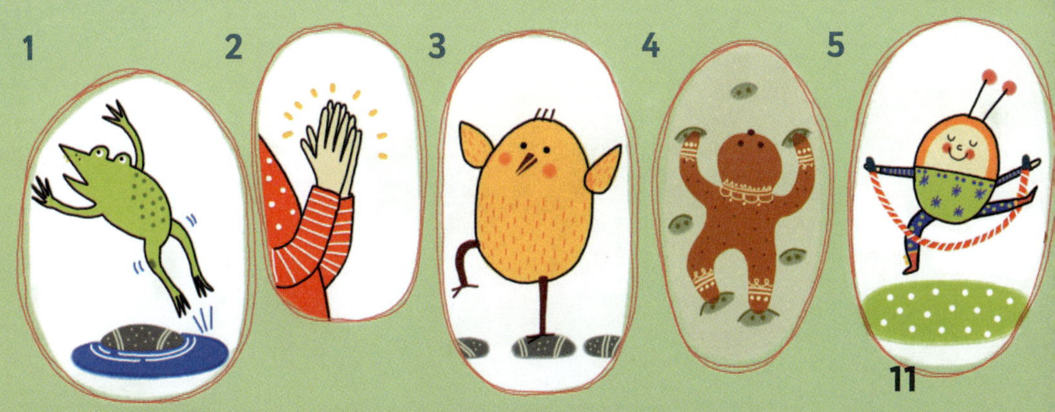

8 The old woman, the old man and the cow run after the gingerbread man. But the gingerbread man doesn't stop. He runs faster and faster.

Soon he sees a horse. ‘Neigh!’ says the horse. ‘Stop! Come here. I’m hungry.’ But again, the gingerbread man doesn’t stop. He runs faster and faster. And now the horse runs after him.

Look at the picture and find: a banana, an apple, strawberries, a pear and grapes.

9 The old woman, the old man, the cow and the horse run after the gingerbread man.

10 *I've got two little legs*
I can run, run, run!
You can't catch me
This is fun, fun, fun!

Look and find.

How many rabbits are there? ☐

How many fish are there? ☐

How many frogs are there? ☐

How many foxes are there? ☐

11 The gingerbread man thinks he is clever. But soon he meets a fox. 'Hello,' says the fox. 'I'm not hungry. I don't want to eat you. I want to talk to you.' But the gingerbread man doesn't stop. He runs and runs. The fox runs and runs too.

Soon the gingerbread man arrives at a river. 'Oh no! I can't swim!' says the gingerbread man. 'How can I cross the river?'

The fox arrives and says 'I can swim. I can help you.'

Label the parts of the fox.

tail • back • nose • mouth

12 'You can sit on my tail,' says the fox.
'Thank you,' says the gingerbread man.
He sits on the fox's tail. The fox begins to swim.

'Oh no! My legs are in the water,' says the gingerbread man.
'You can sit on my back,' says the fox.
'Thank you,' says the gingerbread man.
He sits on the fox's back. The fox swims across the river.

13 'Oh no! My arms are in the water!' says the gingerbread man.
'You can sit on my nose,' says the fox.
'Thank you,' says the gingerbread man.
He jumps on the fox's nose.

But… oh no! The fox throws the gingerbread man up, up, up in the air.

The fox opens his mouth and the gingerbread man goes down, down, down… into the fox's mouth… GULP!

I'm more

_ _ _ _ _ _
♥ ∞ ☆ ☾ ☆ 🍦

than you!

C ♥	V ☾
E ☆	R 🍦
L ∞	

The fox runs home and sings…

14 *You can run, run, run,*
as fast as you can.
But you're not clever,
little gingerbread man.

A gingerbread man bookmark

You need:
- cardboard
- pens or paints
- buttons
- coloured paper
- a wooden stick
- glue

1 Draw the shape of a gingerbread man or a gingerbread woman.

2 Cut out the shape.

3 Decorate your gingerbread man. You can use paints, buttons, stickers...

4 Attach a wooden stick to your gingerbread man.

Your bookmark is ready!

You can use your bookmark to act out the story, too!

Let's act!

Scene 1

NARRATOR This is a story about a gingerbread man. One day an old woman makes a gingerbread man.

OLD WOMAN I'm hungry. What can I make? I know! I can make a gingerbread man.

OLD MAN Good idea!

NARRATOR So the woman makes a gingerbread man.

GINGERBREAD MAN [*arrives and waves*] Hello! I'm the gingerbread man. I've got a head, two eyes, a nose, a mouth, two arms and two legs.

Scene 2

NARRATOR The old woman puts the gingerbread man in the oven.

OLD MAN Mmm, I'm hungry!

GINGERBREAD MAN [*shouts*] Help, help! Open the door!

OLD WOMAN What's that noise?

NARRATOR The old woman opens the oven. The gingerbread man jumps out and runs across the kitchen.

OLD MAN + OLD WOMAN Hey, stop! Come here! We're hungry! We want to eat you.

NARRATOR But the gingerbread man doesn't stop. He runs and runs and sings…

GINGERBREAD MAN [*runs on the spot*]

CAST [*sing together*]
Run, run, as fast as you can.
You can't catch me. I'm the gingerbread man!

Scene 3

NARRATOR The gingerbread man runs and soon he sees a cow.

COW 'Moo!' I'm hungry. I want to eat you! Stop!

GINGERBREAD MAN Oh no! I can't stop.

CAST [*sing together*]
Run, run, as fast as you can.
You can't catch me. I'm the gingerbread man!

NARRATOR The old woman, the old man and the cow run after the gingerbread man.

Scene 4

NARRATOR The gingerbread man runs faster and faster. Soon he sees a horse.

HORSE Neigh! Hello! I'm hungry. Come here.

GINGERBREAD MAN Oh no. You can't eat me.

CAST [*sing together*]
Run, run, as fast as you can.
You can't catch me. I'm the gingerbread man!

NARRATOR Now the old woman, the old man, the cow and the horse run after the gingerbread man.

GINGERBREAD MAN Ha, ha! You can't catch me!

CAST [*sing together*]
I've got two little legs
I can run, run, run!
You can't catch me
This is fun, fun, fun!

Scene 5

NARRATOR The gingerbread man thinks he is clever. But next he meets a fox.

FOX Hello! Who are you?

GINGERBREAD MAN Hello. I'm the gingerbread man. Are you hungry?

FOX No, I'm not hungry. I don't want to eat you. I want to talk to you.

GINGERBREAD MAN I can't stop. Bye-bye!

NARRATOR The gingerbread man runs and runs.

Scene 6

NARRATOR The gingerbread man arrives at a river.

GINGERBREAD MAN Oh no! I can't swim! How can I cross the river?

FOX I can swim. I can help you. You can sit on my tail.

GINGERBREAD MAN Thank you.

NARRATOR The fox begins to swim.

GINGERBREAD MAN Oh no, my legs are in the water.

FOX You can sit on my back.

GINGERBREAD MAN Thank you.

NARRATOR But…

GINGERBREAD MAN Oh no, my arms are in the water.

FOX You can sit on my nose.

GINGERBREAD MAN Thank you!

NARRATOR But, oh no! The fox is clever. He throws the gingerbread man up, up, up and the gingerbread man goes down, down, down…

FOX GULP! Yummy!

NARRATOR The fox runs home and sings…

CAST [*sing together*]
You can run, run, run,
as fast as you can.
But you're NOT clever,
little gingerbread man!

Activities – Play time

1 Put the story in the correct order.

a 

b 

c 

d 

e 

f 

1 The old woman makes a gingerbread man.

2 The gingerbread man says 'Help! Open the door!'

3 The old woman and the old man run after the gingerbread man.

4 A cow wants to eat the gingerbread man.

5 A horse wants to eat the gingerbread man.

6 A clever fox tricks the gingerbread man!

2 **Find the actions in the wordsearch. Then use the other letters to find the hidden sentence.**

T	H	S	J	E
F	O	K	U	X
C	L	I	M	B
L	C	P	P	A
A	N	H	O	P
P	S	W	I	M

_ _ _   _ _ _ _

_ _ _   _ _ _ _ _.

3 **True or false?**

		T	F
1	The old woman makes a gingerbread girl.	☐	☐
2	The old woman and the old man are hungry.	☐	☐
3	The gingerbread man walks slowly.	☐	☐
4	The cow says 'I want to eat you.'	☐	☐
5	Next he meets a sheep.	☐	☐
6	The horse wants to eat the gingerbread man.	☐	☐
7	The gingerbread man can swim.	☐	☐
8	A fish eats the gingerbread man.	☐	☐

4 Find and circle the words that rhyme.

1 man	cow	can	eat
2 river	fox	woman	box
3 climb	stop	swim	hop

5 The gingerbread man can run. What about you? What can you do? Use the ideas in the box.

swim · ride a bike · draw · play tennis
cook · do judo · speak Spanish

I can... ________________

____

I can't... ________________

____

6 Think about the story. What can we learn from the gingerbread man?

Is it OK to trust everyone?

____

Is it OK to think you are more clever than others?

____

7 Find the parts of the body.

_ _ _ _

_ _ _ _

_ _ _ _ _

_ _ _ _

8 Think of a different ending for the story.

The gingerbread man arrives at a river.

____

____.

9 **Do you like the story? Draw the gingerbread man's face. Then colour him.**

😁 = I love the story!

🙂 = I like the story.

😐 = I don't like the story.